I0617167

Learning to Live:

Life Skills for ALL Ages

Written by: *Tracy M. Dayment*

Inspired by: *Diana Aurora*

Illustrated by: *Emily Boyer*

DAYMENT
LEGACY BOOKS

Copyright © 2023 by Tracy M. Dayment

All rights reserved. No part of this book may be reproduced in any form or used in any matter without written permission of the copyright owner except for use of quotations in a book review.

ISBN: 979-8-9900768-1-5

For my daughter Diana Aurora, without you being an inspiration every day, I would lose out on remembering my own dreams. I will continue to advocate for you for life; you will always be my baby girl.

To my psychic who told me I would one day write a children's book and I laughed at her. I apologize.

Table of Contents

Book Inspiration:

One of my favorite classes in high school was "Independent Living". In this class we had to pretend to live real life with a job, apartment, and how to write checks. While I like to think I did take away some life lessons, I don't feel it went very in depth or prepared me for the future, but that class did always stick with me.

Fast forward twenty plus years and I have my own daughter. A beautiful sixteen-year-old girl with Autism and other challenges. I don't know if she will truly ever be able to live on her own, but I want her to grasp these tools. She does learn a lot of skills while at school in her special education classes, but she forgets just as easily as she learns. With this book I have included learning, review, and mastery pages. It's "easy" to learn something, but can you remember it a week from now, how about a month from now? With this workbook, the goal is to have the answers there. Even if you were to forget how to do something, you can see how you did it before. I have refused to put an age limit on this book. It's really a great tool for anyone; my best friend's six-year-old son and her twenty two-year old stepson can learn from each activity just the same.

Book Layout:

      This book is meant to work in any direction you want, either skip around or go in order. However, it is highly suggested to begin with the Future Living section, which I will go into more detail in Chapter Two. Each life skill is set up to learn, review, and master. It may take a couple times to review before mastering is accomplished, and that's okay. Each person is totally different. Do not get frustrated if you don't get it right away. I'm not a fan of the phrase "practice makes perfect", because that's not true at all. However, practicing will allow for a better understanding which is really the end goal. As I mentioned, and will continue to mention, each person is totally different. Go at your own pace. There may be some activities not included in this book that are important for your child or yourself to know. At the end of the book are additional pages you can use for extra activities that are important to you and your family but were not included in the book. I do ask, when this book is completed, please do not discard it. Store the book in a handy location to continue to use for future reference.

Chapter Two:
Future Living Project

The Project

We will start with a whole fictitious world. In this world the learner will have a job, the responsibility of weekly and monthly bills, and be able to save money. This project gives the opportunity to learn how to count money along with the very essential tool of money management. I bought fake money to make the project more fun. This money looks real (wow, does it look real!), but because of this it's easier for my daughter to learn and understand what real money is like. I highly recommend getting a special wallet for this project, especially if you get the real looking money. Don't want to accidentally pass along fake money to stores! If you don't want to go out and buy money, taking money from a board game around the house, or cutting pieces of paper with money increments will also work. You can be as creative as you want.

A Bill Pay Checklist is included in this chapter. This project is set to go on for a full year. This will help grasp money management and to know that bills aren't just due once, they are a recurring activity. As most adults do not start out with absolutely no money, I allowed my daughter to begin her life with $2000. I must have felt generous that day. Be sure to check the box after the bill has been paid, don't want to end up double paying! There are additional lines for extra bills that may come around. I'm very forgetful when it comes to knowing when these things are due. Let's face it, with life going on, it's not the top thing on my mind. I found setting these activities on a calendar or electronic calendar helps a lot. Plus, if the child sees it, they can also remember their bills are due. The Bill Pay research can become overwhelming, such as all bills. If you get too overwhelmed, take a break. This is supposed to be a fun project. So, with all of that said…. let's get started!

Job/Career:

We chose to have a career. It makes the game a bit more fun. My daughter wants to be a hair stylist, so I looked up the average salary of a hair stylist online. I went on the lower side because someone just starting their career isn't going to be making a really good salary at first. Add up the amount per month they would make, but don't forget to take out taxes! Welcome to the real world. For example, we figure $20 per hour for full time, with fictious taxes coming out would be $2400 per month. You can decide if they will be getting paid weekly, biweekly, bimonthly, etc. We set up biweekly, so every other Friday she will be making $1200. Now the tricky part, living within those means.

Mortgage/Rent:

Step one: Decide if there will be a roommate or if you are living on your own. Remember, having a roommate means splitting half of those bills. A much more reasonable cost.

Step two: Go online, check out a few houses or apartments and see what there is out there. Your rent or mortgage payment should be no more than 30% of your monthly income. How quickly we find out that roommate may be needed! Find an apartment or house that is in a decent area, affordable, and any extras you may want in it. Just remember, as a young adult starting out, you may have to give up some things that were important to you. For example, having a washer and dryer in the unit, or the apartment complex not allowing animals. As you get older, those are things you can work towards, but it's the time to realize that you can't necessarily have everything you want.

Homeowners/Renters Insurance:

Well, here's your first bill you probably didn't even think about. Why do you need this insurance? What will happen if your neighbor burns down the entire complex? What will happen if someone breaks into your house? This insurance is a must to protect yourself and all your belongings. I've heard too many stories of someone's house burning to the ground, losing everything, and they didn't even have insurance to help them out. They literally lose everything and become homeless. A little bit of protection will go a long way.

Car Loan:

Assuming you don't live near public transportation or just want the independence of a car. Again, another compromise so early on. As someone just starting out, you can't blow a huge amount of money on the newest car, truck, or SUV with all the bells and whistles. Go online and find a car that will not break down and the monthly payments will be affordable. Most car websites have great loan calculators as well. My daughter's dream car has always been a red Dodge Ram. She decided to settle on a gray Chevy Trax for this project. Quite a difference. No one is saying you can never earn your dream car, but it's something you'll need to continue to work for and save for.

If you choose to go with no car, don't forget to pay for public transportation!

Car Insurance:

It is law to have car insurance if you have a car. Online you can get a quick quote of how much insurance will be for your age (we assumed my daughter was about 23 for this project), for the type of car, and for the area you live in. Remember to use the zip code of where your apartment or house is in.

Gas:

This car thing just keeps adding up! Decide if you will be driving often, normal mileage, or low mileage. Come up with an average weekly cost for gas. This will obviously vary in real life, but an average is a good start.

Cell Phone:

These days a cell phone is as much of a necessity as a good pen. They are not cheap and require to be paid monthly. If you already have one, you can figure out your portion of that bill. If you don't, you can go to any wireless company to figure out how much it would cost.

Electricity:

Yay! Something that can be split with the roommate if you have one. Read that apartment listing and see if it's included. You may have lucked out of a bill. If not, try to get the average cost in your area. My family lives in Arizona. We have insanely high electricity bills in the summer for much-needed air conditioning, but our winter bills are super low when we refuse to turn on the heat. In the end, it all averages out, so just take the average you can find.

Water:

Another utility you can share with the roommate. Just like electricity, make sure it's not already included in rent, and if it is, phew, you get to pass on this bill! If it isn't, take the average water bill in your area. You can do a quick search online.

Internet:

This can also be split with the roommate. Now you can see why it may be worth having one. This may be included in the rent these days. Again, if you have to pay it monthly, take an average for your area.

Health Insurance:

Yes, another insurance! If you are working for a larger company, they may pay a portion of your insurance and you pay the rest. It can still be pricey, but definitely worth having. This can come out of your paychecks, or you can pay it separately each pay period or a one lump monthly payment. Insurance varies so much in cost. My best advice is to ask a couple, family and friends how much their insurance costs and take that average. As an individual it's usually not too much, it's when you start adding a spouse or kids that it really adds up.

Groceries:

I don't know about you, but I really enjoy food. Healthy food, junk food, it's all good. There will be a whole chapter on groceries and your bill will vary every week. Get an idea of how much you should budget. Everyone is different, so it's hard to search online for this information. Are you into eating healthy, organic, and vegan? Well, that will cost you more. Are you into junk food? That will cost less, but becoming unhealthy will cost you more in the long run. Find a happy medium and be realistic thinking about the types of food you would buy.

Extra Spending:

I'm a homebody, so for me, I don't need much to go out. However, my daughter is young and still likes to be out any chance she can get. Out to dinner, out to the movies, out shopping. This stuff adds up and it adds up quick. In order to keep that social life, money must be put aside to make it happen. The other day my family grabbed some fast food as we were too lazy that night to make dinner. I charged my daughter 10 fake dollars to eat her meal. That's the best way she can truly feel how much eating out can add up.

Savings:

Do you think you can manage to add in some extra savings after all those bills? If you are spending correctly, you will have some money left over to save. You never know when you will need to dip into the savings for an emergency or maybe you will have a vacation you are saving up for. My husband and I have joked that the next time my daughter does something she should be punished for, along with extra chores, we can tell her that she just blew out a car tire and now owes $200. While we haven't actually done that, it's not that bad of an idea. Unexpected expenses come up, that's a part of life. Good life lessons. We put the savings in a separate envelope, so it does not get spent and it doesn't go into the bank to never be seen again.

Bank:

The bank is where all the paycheck money will come from and where all the bill payments will be collected. I keep a nice small box of this money. Assuming a child is the one using the book, don't let them have access to that box. Nothing like a bank robbery on your hands.

Bill Pay Checklist

Name:
Start Date:
Job Title:
Salary per month:

	Bill	Date Due	Amount	Month 1	2	3	4	5	6	7	8	9	10	11	12
1	Mortgage/Rent														
2	Homeowners/Renters Insurance														
3	Car Loan														
4	Car Insurance														
5	Gas														
6	Cell Phone														
7	Electricity														
8	Water														
9	Internet														
10	Groceries														
11	Extra Spending														
12	Savings														
13															
14															
15															
16															
17															
18															
19															
20															

Groceries are a big part of living. The human body cannot last without food, not to mention food is so tasty. I do assume we have started out with the essentials of spices and condiments, aluminum foil, etc. However, if you are truly about ready to live on your own, start buying things like this a little at a time, so when you do venture out, you will have what you need.

Pick a day of the week; Fridays are our chosen date. Look at the ad of the store you enjoy going to or will you be heading to multiple stores for all items and spending your weekend traveling to pick everything up. Make a shopping list. Remember, you need food for complete meals. Example, chicken, maybe you want a sauce to go with it, a side dish, a drink, maybe you want to splurge on a dessert. Don't forget other essentials like toothpaste and shampoo! Most stores these days have the option to shop online. I find this tool the easiest to fake shop as it will add everything up and calculate tax. If you don't go through the shopping online portion of the store's website, you can add everything up on your own, but don't forget a tax estimate.

I would highly recommend shopping weekly. However, if you're a monthly shopper, have at it. If you do stick to the weekly schedule, on the Bill Pay Checklist, separate the checkbox for that month and bill into 4. Then you'll have 4 weeks to add a checkmark once completed. Print several copies of this checklist for your own use. Maybe even use Google or Alexa to help you out. So many different options.

Grocery **List**

Date to shop: _____

LEARNING TO LIVE:
Life Skills for ALL Ages

Don't forget!

Meat • Bread • Sugar • Creamer • Milk • Butter • Tea

Cereal • Snacks • Drinks • Fruits • Vegetables

Important Basics

This chapter talks about the important basic information that every child and adult should know. Without having this information memorized, a dangerous situation may arise. These items took my daughter a very long time to learn. It was something we had to work on repeatedly. Repetition is key. Even once mastered, it would be highly suggested to go over it again just to make sure the child did not forget.

Home address:

Knowing your home address is a must. It's needed in an emergency situation and even if you're telling your friend where you live. I was at an event and was surprised by how many teenagers did not know what their address was. They may have known the street name, but not the entire thing.

My home address is:

_____

_____

_____

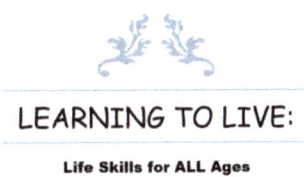

LEARNING TO LIVE:

Life Skills for ALL Ages

Topic: Home Address

Date Learned: _____

Date Reviewed: _____

Date Mastered: _____

What I learned:

_____

_____

_____

_____

_____

_____

_____

_____

_____

_____

_____

_____

_____

_____

_____

_____

_____

_____

Addressing an envelope:

For the post office to deliver a letter, card, bill, or package, the address must be written correctly. It must be kept neat, easy to read, and spelled correctly.

Your name (the sender) must be in the upper left-hand corner. Listed as 3 vertical lines with name, street address, city state and zip. State may be abbreviated.

Your friend's name (the recipient) must be in the middle of the envelope. Listed as 3 vertical lines. Listed as 3 vertical lines with name, street address, city state and zip. State may be abbreviated.

The stamp must be stuck in the upper right-hand corner. Without a stamp the post office will not deliver your item.

Tracy Jackson
123 Main Street
Anywhere, AZ 12345

Stamp

Diana Jackson
321 Center Street
Nowhere, AZ 13245

LEARNING TO LIVE:

Life Skills for ALL Ages

Topic: Address an Envelope (using your own address)

Date Learned: _____

Date Reviewed: _____

Date Mastered: _____

What I learned:

_____

_____

_____

_____

_____

_____

_____

_____

_____

_____

_____

_____

_____

_____

_____

_____

Parent's Phone Number:

With cell phones, it's easy to not have these important numbers memorized. However, what happens when the phone battery dies? What happens if there's an emergency and the phone is broken or can't be located? It is highly important for every child to have their caregivers' phone number(s) memorized.

Learn the phone number in a rhythm or make up a song. It makes the 10 digits of the number much easier to remember.

Mom's Number: _____

Dad's Number: _____

_____'s Number : _____

_____'s Number : _____

LEARNING TO LIVE:

Life Skills for ALL Ages

Topic: Parent's Phone Number

Date Learned: _____

Date Reviewed: _____

Date Mastered: _____

What I learned:

_____
_____
_____
_____
_____
_____
_____
_____
_____
_____
_____
_____
_____
_____
_____
_____
_____

Social Security Number:

Social Security Numbers are very important to know. However, if in the wrong hands, it can be a dangerous scenario. It is suggested you work on this page with your child if they are at the age of getting a job or sending college applications. This is a very important number, so I will not be leaving a blank spot for it. It's suggested to be a number that is memorized.

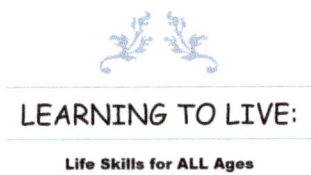

LEARNING TO LIVE:

Life Skills for ALL Ages

Topic: Social Security Number

Date Learned: _____

Date Reviewed: _____

Date Mastered: _____

What I learned:

_____
_____
_____
_____
_____
_____
_____
_____
_____
_____
_____
_____
_____
_____
_____
_____
_____
_____

Signature:

In today's world, cursive (or handwriting) is not often used or taught. However, everyone still needs their own personal signature that is unique to them. While checks may not be written much anymore, a signature will still be needed for important paperwork. Decide whether to include the middle name in full, just the first letter of the middle name, or opt to keep it out completely.

X _____

X _____

X _____

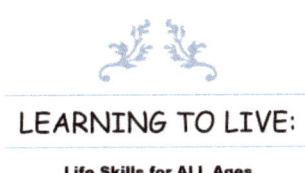

LEARNING TO LIVE:

Life Skills for ALL Ages

Topic: Signature

Date Learned: _____

Date Reviewed: _____

Date Mastered: _____

What I learned:

_____

_____

_____

_____

_____

_____

_____

_____

_____

_____

_____

_____

_____

_____

_____

_____

_____

Place an emergency (911) call:

Emergencies can come when they're least expected. Knowing not only how to place this very important call calmly, but also relay the information that was mentioned earlier in this chapter will give the emergency services everything they need.

Remain calm: It is imperative to remain calm. This will allow the first responders on the phone to understand what the emergency is. Speak slowly and clearly. Advise what the emergency is, the address where the emergency is (we will use the home address), and the call back phone number in case the phone is disconnected. Do some role play, see below to get started.

Answer the following script to get started, then do some extra role play on your own.

Operator: 911, what is your emergency?

Answer: _____

Operator: What is the address of the emergency?

Answer: _____

Operator: What phone number are you calling from?

Answer: _____

LEARNING TO LIVE:

Life Skills for ALL Ages

Topic: Placing an emergency (911) call

Date Learned: _____

Date Reviewed: _____

Date Mastered: _____

What I learned:

_____

_____

_____

_____

_____

_____

_____

_____

_____

_____

_____

_____

_____

_____

_____

_____

_____

Kitchen

The kitchen is one of the most important rooms in the house. Everyone needs to eat and it's good to learn how to feed ourselves without having to depend on anyone else.

I have chosen simple meals with step-by-step directions. Feel free to add recipes to this to keep for future use as well.

It would be a great idea to keep a folder of several recipes the child is able to make. This will build confidence in the kitchen. After the child feels comfortable in the kitchen, have them pick a day of the week that they will be responsible for cooking dinner for the family. This will build confidence in cooking and will hopefully lead them to challenge themselves later with more difficult recipes.

Kitchen Safety:

The kitchen is where masterpieces can be made. However, it can also be one of the most dangerous places in the house. Be sure to also have safety in mind.

• Never point a knife at anyone including yourself. Hold your knife with the sharp edge facing down.

• Remember stove burners can remain hot even after you turn it off. Do not touch the burners, or even the pans with your hands. Use well-fitting oven mitts when holding hot items.

• Do not run in the kitchen.

• Keep an eye on your cooking. While you don't have to watch your item every second, you do need to keep a watch. Boiling water can overflow, and food can burn.

• Wear clothing that is not too loose and does not have hanging strings.

• Do not use the same cutting board without washing between different raw meats, fruits, and vegetables.

• Do not set a hot glass dish on a wet or cold surface. The glass dish will break. (I learned this one the hard way.)

• Always have a fire extinguisher or a box of baking soda in the kitchen. Be sure whoever is cooking knows where it is located.

LEARNING TO LIVE:

Life Skills for ALL Ages

Topic: Kitchen Safety

Date Learned: _____

Date Reviewed: _____

Date Mastered: _____

What I learned:

_____
_____
_____
_____
_____
_____
_____
_____
_____
_____
_____
_____
_____
_____
_____
_____
_____

Simple Cooking – Breakfast: Scrambled Eggs

Tools:
Skillet
Medium Bowl
Spatula
Wisk
Ingredients:
2 Large Eggs
1 Tsp (Teaspoon) milk of your choice
Butter or spray nonstick cooking spray
(Optional) Pepper
Recipe:
1: Crack eggs into medium bowl avoiding getting any shell bits into the bowl.
2: Add milk
3: Wisk eggs and milk together. Add a little pepper if preferred.
4: Spray the skillet with nonstick cooking spray or a little bit of butter
5: Pour eggs into skillet and turn stove heat to medium.
6: Stir eggs with spatula. Move all eggs around until they are mostly firm with a little bit of liquid.
7: Put eggs on plate and enjoy!

Remember kitchen safety; watch yourself around the hot stove and hot pan.

LEARNING TO LIVE:

Life Skills for ALL Ages

Topic: Simple Cooking - Breakfast

Date Learned: _____

Date Reviewed: _____

Date Mastered: _____

What I learned:

_____
_____
_____
_____
_____
_____
_____
_____
_____
_____
_____
_____
_____
_____
_____
_____
_____

Simple Cooking - Lunch: Grilled Cheese

Tools:
Skillet
Butter knife
Spatula
Ingredients:
2 slices of bread
1 Tbsp (Tablespoon) Butter
1-2 slices of American cheese
Recipe:
1: Turn stove to medium heat.
2: Use ¼ Tbsp of butter bottom of bread.
3: Lay buttered side of bread down in the skillet
4: Carefully butter top of bread
5: Top the bread with cheese
6: Butter one side of the other piece of bread and lay it on top of cheese.
7: Butter top of bread.
8: After about 3 minutes, carefully use spatula to lift sandwich, flip the sandwich when the bread is a golden brown.
9: Repeat for other side of bread.
10: Once completed, put on plate and enjoy!

Remember kitchen safety; watch yourself around the hot stove and hot pan.

LEARNING TO LIVE:

Life Skills for ALL Ages

Topic: Simple Cooking - Lunch

Date Learned: _____

Date Reviewed: _____

Date Mastered: _____

What I learned:

_____
_____
_____
_____
_____
_____
_____
_____
_____
_____
_____
_____
_____
_____
_____
_____
_____

Simple Cooking - Dinner: Spaghetti

Tools:
Large Pot
Large Stirring Spoon (I prefer a wooden spoon)
Strainer
Tongs
Ingredients:
Spaghetti noodles
Water
½ Cup Jarred Spaghetti Sauce
Recipe:
1: Fill pot halfway with water
2: Place on stove and turn stove to High heat.
3: When water boils (about 8 minutes there will be lots of fast bubbles), turn the stove to medium heat.
4: Take approximately a palm full of spaghetti noodles and over the pot, break the whole stack in half and drop them in the pot.
5: Let the spaghetti noodles boil for approximately 8 minutes, 9-10 if you like softer noodles. Stir occasionally as they cook.
6: Place strainer in the kitchen sink and extremely carefully pour the noodles and hot water into the strainer.
7: Once all water is out, pour the noodles back in the pot and pour in ½ cup of spaghetti sauce.
8: Use tongs to plate spaghetti and enjoy!

Remember kitchen safety; watch yourself around the hot stove and hot pan.

LEARNING TO LIVE:

Life Skills for ALL Ages

Topic: Simple Cooking - Dinner

Date Learned: _____

Date Reviewed: _____

Date Mastered: _____

What I learned:

_____

_____

_____

_____

_____

_____

_____

_____

_____

_____

_____

_____

_____

_____

_____

_____

_____

Simple Cooking - Dessert: Crispy Rice Treats

Tools:
Baking Dish
Aluminum Foil
Large Pot
Large Stirring Spoon
Rubber Spatula
Ingredients:
Non-Stick Cooking Spray
4 tbsp (tablespoon) of Butter
10 oz (ounce) of Mini Marshmallows
6 cups of Crispy Rice Cereal
1 tsp (teaspoon) of Vanilla Extract
Recipe:
1: Line a baking pan with foil so the edges come over the top about 2 inches.
2: Spray the foil with non-stick cooking spray
3: Add butter to pot and turn stove to medium heat.
4: When butter is melted, pour in marshmallows. Stir occasionally for about 5 minutes. Marshmallows should be smooth. Remove from heat.
5: Add crispy rice cereal to the pot while working quickly and stir with the spatula until all cereal is coated.
6: Pour the pot of cereal into the lined baking sheet.
7: Spray hands with a little non-stick cooking spray and press the cereal across the baking sheet so it's evenly covered.
8: Let them cool for 30 minutes and then cut squares and enjoy!

Remember kitchen safety; watch yourself around the hot stove and hot pan.

LEARNING TO LIVE:

Life Skills for ALL Ages

Topic: Simple Cooking - Dessert

Date Learned: _____

Date Reviewed: _____

Date Mastered: _____

What I learned:

_____
_____
_____
_____
_____
_____
_____
_____
_____
_____
_____
_____
_____
_____
_____
_____
_____

Putting out a grease fire:

As mentioned earlier, kitchens are great to get creative, however they can also be very dangerous. It is important to know what to do in case a grease fire breaks out.

Grease fires occur when grease, oil, or fat on a stovetop or in the oven ignite due to high heat. They can truly happen to anyone. The below instructions must be followed in the exact order.

1. Remain calm.
2. Turn off the stove and/or oven.
3. Cover the pot or pan with a lid.
4. Douse the fire with a fire extinguisher, baking soda, or even salt.

NEVER USE WATER ON A GREASE FIRE.

Using water on a grease fire will cause the fire to spread much quicker and can make a dangerous situation even more dangerous.

If the fire is large or you are unable to put a small fire out, you must exit the house immediately and call 911.

LEARNING TO LIVE:

Life Skills for ALL Ages

Topic: Putting out a grease fire

Date Learned: _____

Date Reviewed: _____

Date Mastered: _____

What I learned:

_____
_____
_____
_____
_____
_____
_____
_____
_____
_____
_____
_____
_____
_____
_____
_____

Building a future can be both an exciting time and a little nerve wracking as well. In this chapter, we will go over several areas that will help kick start your goals. I remember being in high school and was so pressured to pick a career my Junior year. I didn't feel like I was given the right tools to make my decision and was forced to decide what I would do with my life. It's a big decision at just sixteen years old. To those that are undecided, it's okay. It's okay to not have figured out what you would like to do the rest of your life. It's okay to change your mind. I hope this chapter will help give you another outlet to help make those big decisions.

Conducting a job search

Job searches can become overwhelming no matter what type of position you are applying for.

Restaurant/Retail:

You may go into the restaurant or store and ask for an application. You may also want to ask for a manager who can tell you more about the position or possibly the pay. If you are given an application, you can either fill it out while onsite or take it home and bring it back once completed.

Another option would be to go to the restaurant's or store's website. Typically, there is a career section which you can fill out the application online. If going this route, be prepared to be asked several questions by the website about your work ethic. Oftentimes, companies will use an algorithm to sift through applications. This will allow managers not to have to look at every single application that comes through.

Office or professional positions:

Typically, these positions will be listed on career specific websites. They will not only have you fill out an application online, but also send your resume. Again, it is typical the algorithm will be in place. If you use the same career website for all your job searching, you oftentimes will be allowed to keep your resume on file, which you will be able to run through submitting a bit quicker.

Just like with restaurants and stores, most companies will also have a career section on their own website. This is a great way to apply if there's a specific company you want to work for. Check back often as job opportunities will update.

In this section, type in a couple different key words into a job board search engine. Check to see what comes up for these positions. You may notice your key words are too broad or too specific. Play around with it until you find positions in which you would truly be interested in the future.

LEARNING TO LIVE:

Life Skills for ALL Ages

Topic: Conducting a job search

Date Learned: _____

Date Reviewed: _____

Date Mastered: _____

What I learned:

_____

_____

_____

_____

_____

_____

_____

_____

_____

_____

_____

_____

_____

_____

_____

_____

Filling out a job application:

Some companies, especially those in retail or food service, require an application to be filled out instead of sending a resume. At times you are given the opportunity to interview as soon as the application is filled out. If this is the case, it's even more important to know how to fill out an application on your own.

Project:

Start with the generic application for the "learned" log. Once it comes to "reviewed" and "mastered," select two different companies. Each company has similar yet different questions. It is suggested to print, if possible, the application prior to filling it out (unless you are filling it out for real instead of practice). Either pick up applications from local shops or go to the company website. See the following few pages for the first sample application. Following the application is the "Application Help Guide." This will hopefully help answer any questions.

EMPLOYMENT / JOB APPLICATION

PERSONAL INFORMATION

FULL NAME: _____ DATE: _____

ADDRESS:

_____

_____

E-MAIL: _____ PHONE: _____

SOCIAL SECURITY NUMBER (SSN): _____-_____-_____

DATE AVAILABLE: _____ DESIRED PAY: $_____
☐ HOUR ☐ SALARY

POSITION APPLIED FOR:

_____

EMPLOYMENT DESIRED:
☐ FULL-TIME ☐ PART-TIME ☐ SEASONAL

EMPLOYMENT ELIGIBILITY

ARE YOU LEGALLY ELIGIBLE TO WORK IN THE U.S?
☐ YES ☐ NO*

HAVE YOU EVER WORKED FOR THIS EMPLOYER? ☐ YES* ☐ NO

*IF YES, WRITE THE START AND END DATES:

_____

HAVE YOU EVER BEEN CONVICTED OF A FELONY?
☐ YES* ☐ NO

*IF YES, PLEASE EXPLAIN:

_____

EDUCATION

HIGH SCHOOL: _____

CITY / STATE: _____

FROM: _____ TO: _____

GRADUATE? ☐ YES ☐ NO DIPLOMA: _____

COLLEGE: _____

CITY / STATE: _____

FROM: _____ TO: _____

GRADUATE? ☐ YES ☐ NO DEGREE: _____

OTHER: _____

CITY / STATE: _____

FROM: _____ TO: _____

DEGREE/CERTIFICATION: _____

OTHER: _____

CITY / STATE: _____

FROM: _____ TO: _____

DEGREE/CERTIFICATION: _____

PREVIOUS EMPLOYMENT

EMPLOYER 1:

_____
Company / Individual

E-MAIL: _____

PHONE: _____

ADDRESS:

_____
Street Address   Apt/Suite

_____
City   State   Zip Code

STARTING PAY: $_____ ☐ HOUR ☐ SALARY

ENDING PAY: $_____ ☐ HOUR ☐ SALARY

JOB TITLE: _____

RESPONSIBILITIES: _____

FROM: _____ TO: _____

REASON FOR LEAVING:
_____

EMPLOYER 2:

_____
Company / Individual

E-MAIL: _____

PHONE: _____

ADDRESS:

_____

Street Address   Apt/Suite

_____

City   State   Zip Code

STARTING PAY: $_____ ☐ HOUR ☐ SALARY

ENDING PAY: $_____ ☐ HOUR ☐ SALARY

JOB TITLE: _____

RESPONSIBILITIES: _____

FROM: _____ TO: _____

REASON FOR LEAVING:

_____

EMPLOYER 3:

_____

Company / Individual

E-MAIL: _____

PHONE: _____

ADDRESS:

_____

Street Address   Apt/Suite

_____

City   State   Zip Code

STARTING PAY: $_____ ☐ HOUR ☐ SALARY

ENDING PAY: $_____ ☐ HOUR ☐ SALARY

JOB TITLE: _____

RESPONSIBILITIES: _____

FROM: _____ TO: _____

REASON FOR LEAVING:

_____

REFERENCES
(PROFESSIONAL ONLY)

FULL NAME:

_____
      First   Last

RELATIONSHIP: _____

COMPANY: _____

TITLE: _____

E-MAIL: _____

PHONE: _____

FULL NAME:

_____
      First   Last

RELATIONSHIP: _____

COMPANY: _____

TITLE: _____

E-MAIL: _____

PHONE: _____

FULL NAME:

_____

First   Last

RELATIONSHIP: _____

COMPANY: _____

TITLE: _____

E-MAIL: _____

PHONE: _____

MILITARY SERVICE

ARE YOU A VETERAN? ☐ YES ☐ NO

BRANCH: _____
RANK AT DISCHARGE: _____

FROM: _____ TO: _____

TYPE OF DISCHARGE: _____

IF NOT HONORABLE, PLEASE EXPLAIN:

_____

BACKGROUND CHECK CONSENT

IF ASKED, ARE YOU WILLING TO CONSENT TO A BACKGROUND CHECK?
☐ YES ☐ NO

DISCLAIMER

Applicant understands that this is an Equal Opportunity Employer and committed to excellence through diversity. In order to ensure this application is acceptable, please print or type with the application being fully completed in order for it to be considered.

Please complete each section EVEN IF you decide to attach a resume.

I, the Applicant, certify that my answers are true and honest to the best of my knowledge. If this application leads to my eventual employment, I understand that any false or misleading information in my application or interview may result in my employment being terminated.

SIGNATURE _____

DATE _____

PRINT NAME _____

Application Help Guide:

Full Name:

First, Middle, and Last Name

Date:

Today's Date

Address:

Your current mailing address

Email:

The email they may use to reach out to you.

Phone:

The phone number you can be contacted.

Social Security Number:

This is needed in case you are employed with them.

Date Available:

This question refers to the date you can begin working. The question can be answered in a few different ways. If you do not have any commitments, you may want to write "ASAP" or "As soon as possible". You may also write a specific date you are able to begin work, or if you need to give a current employer proper notice, you may want to write "2 weeks".

Desired Pay:

How much are you hoping to get paid either per hour or salary? Remember what you are worth. If this is your first job, look at what minimum wage is. You can go above that but remember to reach for the stars on this. Many employers, when reviewing applications, will look at this number before anything else and if the amount is way more than they are willing to pay, they will not set up an interview. Do not undercut yourself either. If there are a lot of tough job responsibilities, be sure to keep that in mind and try to find a good middle ground for what you feel you should be paid. Another option would be writing "Open to Discussion" and it can be discussed during an interview.

Employment Desired:

What type of hours are you looking to work per week? Full-time = typically 37+ hours; Part-time = typically less than 32 hours; Seasonal = typically for one season, i.e., a college student may be looking to work during their winter break.

Are you legally eligible to work in the U.S.?
To legally be able to work in the United States, you must be a US citizen with a social security number OR were issued a working VISA if you were born in another country.

Have you ever worked for this employer?
If you have worked for the employer in the past, be sure to check the 'yes' box and explain what your role was along with the dates you were previously employed.

Have you ever been convicted of a felony?
You must be completely honest with this question. If hired, more than likely, the employer will do a background check. If you lie about this question, it will come up. It's always better to be truthful.

Education:
List any, and all, education. If you are currently in high school, fill that out completely, even if you have not completed it yet. Same goes for if you are currently in college.

Previous Employment:

Be sure to list any, and all, previous employment. Be truthful. The employer you are applying for may call the previous employment to check if they would hire you again if given the opportunity.

References:

References are people you give this employer permission to contact. Always ask permission and inform your contact. They need to be aware the employer may call or email them. Typically, good references consist of one or two professional references (past coworker, teacher, etc.) along with a friend that you've known for a while. Be sure you have a good relationship with the people you list. If contacted, they will be the ones to help you get the job opportunity.

Military Service:

If this question is asked, again, be sure to be truthful.

Background Check:

It is completely up to the individual to consent to a background check or not. However, most companies do require these. If you do not consent, please note, a company also has the right to throw the application into a pile that they will never look at.

Disclaimer:

By filling this out, you are advising the employer everything is correct on your application.

Equal Opportunity Employer:

This is an employer that pledges not to discriminate against employees based on race, color, religion, sex, national origin, age, disability or genetic information.

LEARNING TO LIVE:

Life Skills for ALL Ages

Topic: Filling out a job application

Date Learned: _____

Date Reviewed: _____

Date Mastered: _____

What I learned:

_____

_____

_____

_____

_____

_____

_____

_____

_____

_____

_____

_____

_____

_____

_____

_____

_____

Writing a resume

There is no wrong way to write a resume. A resume is what showcases your abilities along with any experience you have had in the past. The most important thing about your resume is to have it stand out. Keep in mind, there may be some positions with hundreds of applicants. Think about if a room was filled with one hundred people, how would the employer pick you. Resumes are always evolving, which means it's best to do a web search of "professional stand out resumes".

Things to include on a resume:

- Phone number and email address
- An objective of the position you are trying to obtain. (If writing a cover letter, skip this step)
- Past employment
- Detailed, but not overly detailed examples of job duties in past employment (written in full sentences
- Volunteer experiences
- It's okay to have 2-3 pages, but do not go more.

Things to NOT include on a resume:

- Your picture
- Misspelled words (always use spell check)

As a person who has reviewed several resumes, please note, if you do not include a phone number, you won't be getting a phone call. When employers are ready to hire, they aren't going to wait to see if you respond to an email. Practice writing a resume that will make you noticeable.

LEARNING TO LIVE:

Life Skills for ALL Ages

Topic: Writing a resume

Date Learned: _____

Date Reviewed: _____

Date Mastered: _____

What I learned:

_____
_____
_____
_____
_____
_____
_____
_____
_____
_____
_____
_____
_____
_____
_____
_____
_____

Interviewing

Filling out an application or resume is the first step but getting a call to schedule an interview is exciting. Below are some things to keep in mind. When scheduling this interview, you need to be looking at your own calendar. You don't want to double book yourself and not be able to make the date and time you committed to. Some employers only have certain dates and time available for interviews. If this is the case, you may need to double book yourself and move your previous engagement. Always show up to the interview you have scheduled. If you do not call ahead of time and do not show for the time scheduled, that can ruin your chances of landing any position at that company. Bigger companies can input whether you have interviewed prior or have missed a scheduled interview.

Receiving a Call:

Prior to sending out resumes or applications, always check your incoming voicemail greeting. Ensure it is appropriate if an employer calls you and you are unable to answer the phone. Always answer your phone professionally with a friendly hello. You never know when you might get that call to set up an interview.

Yay, you landed an interview! Now what?

Do your research:

Research the company and the position you applied for. With this knowledge, you will be able to ask the right questions during the interview.

Dress professionally:

No matter if the interview is in person, a video call, or even over the phone. Dressing professionally will make you feel better about yourself which in turn will help you interview better.

Arrival time:

Always arrive early, but not too early. If you are unsure of where the employer is located, you may want to take a test drive to the building beforehand. Always allow for extra time due to traffic, construction, or the unknown. If you end up super early, it's a good idea to stay in your car for a while and pass some of the time. Arriving too early can be a stressor to an interviewer. Always arrive or check in with five to ten minutes to spare. It will show the

interviewer that you are prompt and ready to go. If for some reason you are not able to be there on time, call the interviewer as soon as you can to inform them.

Always remain professional:

Arrive with a pen and pad of paper along with a copy of your resume. Always keep a smile on your face. Remain truthful during the interview. Do not talk badly about ex coworkers or a former employer. Remember you may be trying to beat out another hundred applicants. The interview is your time to shine. Explain what experience you are bringing and why you should be the one they chose for this position. Have a couple questions ready to ask at the end of the interview. Do not interrupt the interviewer. Be friendly and good luck with your interview!

Follow up:

If you have the interviewer's email address, it would be great to thank them for the opportunity. If you have not heard from the interviewer by the date they had originally set forth, call or email to inquire. Showing you are interested in this position can go a long way.

In this section, interview a family member who already has a job. See how they would answer some interview questions (use a search engine to find commonly used questions). Pay attention to how they answer these questions, would you give them the job if you were the hiring manager? Once you get the "Reviewed" part, have the roles reverse. Allow them to ask you whatever questions they feel appropriate, that may be in an interview. Talk with them to see where they feel you can improve or maybe you are answering them perfectly. Remember, it's not only about the questions being asked, but also about your personality and your professionalism.

LEARNING TO LIVE:

Life Skills for ALL Ages

Topic: Interviewing

Date Learned: _____

Date Reviewed: _____

Date Mastered: _____

What I learned:

_____

_____

_____

_____

_____

_____

_____

_____

_____

_____

_____

_____

_____

_____

_____

_____

_____

Write a professional email:

There are quite a few reasons why you may want to write a professional email. Whether you are following up on an interview or even if you have a complaint to a cookie company, remaining professional is always key. Think about this, if you were in a customer service position and there are two complaints about the same exact problem, which person would you help first. The one that is yelling and screaming at you, even if it's through an email, or the one that is polite and shares their concern while keeping their cool composure. You'll obviously need to help both of them since that would be your job, the professional one will be a lot easier to deal with.

• Start with a subject line that is to the point

• Address them appropriately. Do not use casual language if being professional (like Hey or Hi), use "Dear" followed by their name, or if you don't know who will be reading the email, "To whom it may concern" will do the trick.

• Keep the email to the point of what you are wanting to say without going off on different tangents.

• Make it easy to read. Use indentations, appropriate spaces, no emojis or slang, keep text a simple color like black or dark blue, and don't use words that are large where the reader will need a dictionary.

• Be kind and thankful, not over dramatic or silly, yet be sure you do use your own personality.

• If you have spoken to this person before, be sure to include some points as they may have had several similar communications with other people.

• Use an appropriate signature closer such as "Sincerely", "Best Regards", or "Thank you".

• Reread. Always reread what you have written. Make sure your point came across clearly and it makes sense. Also, use this time to fix any grammar and spelling mistakes. You may want to consider using a spell and grammar check in your email program.

Now that you have the basics to follow, it's time to try it out. For the "Learned" section, try writing a professional email to a fictious employer you are wanting to follow up with after an interview.

For the "Reviewed" section, write an email, complaint or compliment, to a fictious company regarding an item in your pantry.

Now that you are at the "Mastered" section, write an actual email (or even a letter in the same format) and thank a company you had good customer service with. Many companies only hear complaints if something has gone wrong. It would make their day to hear a compliment. Be sure to include an employee name if you have that information so they can be acknowledged appropriately.

LEARNING TO LIVE:

Life Skills for ALL Ages

Topic: Write a professional email

Date Learned: _____

Date Reviewed: _____

Date Mastered: _____

What I learned:

_____
_____
_____
_____
_____
_____
_____
_____
_____
_____
_____
_____
_____
_____
_____
_____
_____
_____

Professionalism at a business meeting:

Business meetings, no matter the position you obtain, can come around daily, weekly, monthly, or even can be unexpected. Sometimes these meetings may be lunch at a restaurant, and other times they may be at the office throughout the busy day. It is always important to remain professional during these meetings, or really at your job regardless of a meeting.

If wanting to move up in your career, a business, more often than not, will choose someone that remains professional to promote over someone that may know the job better yet lacks professionalism.

Just like during an interview, you will want to dress for success. That does not mean you need to break out the 3-piece suit or the formal gown, but be sure your clothing is within company standards, clean, and free of holes.

Language is a big factor. If you are cussing throughout the meeting, it will sound as if you are upset or do not know how to speak properly. Ask questions throughout the meeting to show your interest but be sure you're not asking what they have already stated. Doing so will make it sound like you were not paying attention.

To practice sounding professional at a business meeting, have a conversation regarding any subject with your parent or friend. Prior to the conversation, advise your family or friend about this chapter. They will then be able to give appropriate advice along with pointers once the conversation is over. Be open to their feedback as the person you chose to have this conversation with should have your best interest at heart. Take that feedback and work on those items for your reviewed and mastered sections. Sometimes professionalism comes with time, but if you continually work on this, it will be easy to achieve.

LEARNING TO LIVE:

Life Skills for ALL Ages

Topic: Professionalism at a business meeting

Date Learned: _____

Date Reviewed: _____

Date Mastered: _____

What I learned:

_____

_____

_____

_____

_____

_____

_____

_____

_____

_____

_____

_____

_____

_____

_____

_____

Deciding on college:

With so many unknowns as the end of high school nears, there are several big decisions on the horizon. What will I major in, will I be more suited for community college or a university, how will I possibly pay for college, is college even something I want to do? These questions along with many others may be floating around in your head. Most importantly, don't cut yourself short. You can do whatever you want to with hard work,

In no way am I going to tell you what is right for your path. Everyone is uniquely themselves and no one path is right for everyone.

Helpful tips:

• Choose a major or career that makes you happy. Something you enjoy doing or learning about. If you find yourself unsure, that is perfectly normal.

• Happiness is the most important, in my opinion, however in order to be able to live, you need to ensure the career you choose has a healthy livable salary as well. Do your research on a few careers to compare what can check the box of happiness and salary.

• Take general education classes first so if you change your mind, you haven't wasted any time.

• Compare the local community college vs up to 3 universities and check tuition, classes and times offered, and even speak to a counselor who can help guide you in the right direction.

This section will be a little different than the ones before. Rather than "Date Learned" it changed to "Top 3 Careers". Pick 3 career choices you believe would be interesting to work the rest of your working life. Once chosen, write them down, and do a little research. Besides salary, you will want to check the future opportunities in this position. What is the outlook 20 or 30 years from now? What is the current job market like for these careers? What colleges are best for this career choice? Do you know someone currently in this career choice? If so, talk with them and ask about their experiences.

Rather than "Date Reviewed", it changed to "Top College Choices". List a community college and up to 3 other colleges you may be considering. Do they offer classes that will help you get to your goal? If there are two similar programs with slightly different degrees, which one will better suit your needs? What is tuition and possibly room and board? Are there extra curriculars on campus that you would also enjoy? What is the process to apply to get into these schools? Set a time to talk to a college representative and, if possible, schedule a tour. While on campus, take the time to talk to other college students and see what experiences they have had,

Rather than "Date Mastered" it will be your "Final Decisions". Do not rush to get to this point. Take your time. It is common to feel pressured and stressed, but this is your life and your decision. Many people end up going back to college years later in life because they changed their paths. It's okay. It will always be okay. Be genuine to yourself.

LEARNING TO LIVE:

Life Skills for ALL Ages

Topic: Deciding on college

Top 3 Career Choices:

_____

Top College Choices:

_____

Final Decisions:

_____

What I learned:

_____
_____
_____
_____
_____
_____
_____
_____
_____
_____
_____
_____
_____
_____

College Admissions:

Congratulations! You've decided on what it is you want to pursue. Some colleges are tougher to get into than others. You may want to send an application to several different colleges or maybe you are wanting to take your chances and only apply to one. I am going to assume you took a college tour of your selections. This means, you may already have the admission application information already. If not, you will want to speak to a college representative to get that information. Many have application fees; some require letters for you to write. Each college is different from the next. Be sure you gather all necessary information prior to sending your application. You would hate to be denied after spending the application fee because you forgot a step.

Even if you are not required to write a letter, it is my suggestion you write a letter to yourself. Tell your future self why you want to attend that college, why you want to major in that program, why it's so important to you. Life at college can be difficult and it would be a great reflection to read on a tough day. Remind yourself you are doing great things and for what reasons you have chosen.

LEARNING TO LIVE:

Life Skills for ALL Ages

Topic: College Admissions

Date Learned: _____

Date Reviewed: _____

Date Mastered: _____

What I learned:

_____
_____
_____
_____
_____
_____
_____
_____
_____
_____
_____
_____
_____
_____
_____
_____
_____
_____
_____

College Costs:

College costs are a huge deciding factor for college. Some people may qualify for loan assistance, some will be able to get full scholarships, some are struggling to figure out how they will pay for college. It's no secret, college is expensive. Remember you are doing this for you and trying to better yourself for a career you will love.

There are hundreds of thousands of scholarships to apply for. Some are school specific; some can be used anywhere. This is one of the most important items to research. If there's "free" money available, do your best to try to obtain it. Just like college applications, it is very important you don't miss any steps that are needed to apply.

Check with financial aid at the college. They are the experts and can walk you through what paying for college will look like. Again, your college experience is for you, you are unique, your situation is unique, advisors will be more than happy to help. This is why they are there, do not be afraid to talk to them.

LEARNING TO LIVE:

Life Skills for ALL Ages

Topic: College Costs

Date Learned: _____

Date Reviewed: _____

Date Mastered: _____

What I learned:

_____

_____

_____

_____

_____

_____

_____

_____

_____

_____

_____

_____

_____

_____

_____

_____

_____

*This chapter is filled with my personal suggestions, in no way am I giving financial advice.

What you need to know about general finances is discussed in this chapter. Somethings you may use often and others just on occasion, however it's all very important information to know. I will say this several times throughout this chapter. In no way is any of this book financial advice. These are some of my suggestions. To receive personalized advice, seek out a financial advisor or similar.

Using an ATM (or in store money back option):

As many young kids may not realize, you have to have money in your checking or savings account to be able to use your debit card. It's a hard truth they will eventually learn.

This seems like a weird life skill to learn, yet a very important reminder. When opening your account and receiving your card, usually there is a minimum balance you need to keep. Every bank will have their own rules and should be discussed while opening the account.

The main reason this is here is for safety. It seems easy to pull up to an ATM, take money, and go.

• Always look over your shoulder and make sure no one is watching.

• Always cover your hand as you input your PIN number. (No one but you should have this information)

• Once finished, put your money away in your wallet or wherever you keep money prior to leaving the area.

• Make sure you have the money to take out. You don't want to have to pay overdraft fees.

All these tips above also apply if you are getting money back from the store cash register. Even if you are not getting any money back and are just using it, make sure no one is watching you input your information. Theft is a scary thing and always do what you can do to prevent it from happening to you.

LEARNING TO LIVE:

Life Skills for ALL Ages

Topic: Using an ATM

Date Learned: _____

Date Reviewed: _____

Date Mastered: _____

What I learned:

_____

_____

_____

_____

_____

_____

_____

_____

_____

_____

_____

_____

_____

_____

_____

_____

_____

Write a check:

It seems that checks are a thing of the past, however, they are still used on occasion and it's important to know how to use them.

Never write a check for more money than you have in your account. Banks will always charge a hefty fee, called a returned check fee, if it comes back when there was no money or not enough money in the account.

```
                                                          10735

                                      DATE_____

PAY TO THE                                          $_____
ORDER OF _____
_____ DOLLARS

MEMO_____
  ⑈⑆⑇123000123⑈⑇456 007890 0⑈       _____
```

Check number: Located in top right corner (in this case it's 10735)

Date: Today's date, including year

Pay to the order of: This is the person or company you are writing the check to.

$: The amount of the check in numbers with the decimal, i.e., $149.53

Dollars: The blank part of this line is filled out with the dollar amount written out. The 'cents' should be written as a fraction, is. one hundred forty-nine and 53/100.

Memo: This is an optional line to fill out so you can remember what the check was for, i.e.. Electric Bill.

Blank Line: This is at the bottom and is reserved for your signature.

The numbers at the bottom of the check are your routing number, checking account number, and check number.

On the back of the check, there will be a place for the "pay to the order of" person can sign, called "Endorse Here". Never sign or write below the line as called out.

ENDORSE HERE

DO NOT WRITE, STAMP, OR SIGN BELOW THIS LINE

RESERVED FOR FINANCIAL INSTITUTION USE

SECURITY FEATURES

• Microprinting around border on face

• Laid lines on back

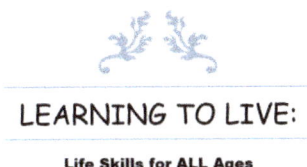

LEARNING TO LIVE:

Life Skills for ALL Ages

Topic: Write a check

Date Learned: _____

Date Reviewed: _____

Date Mastered: _____

What I learned:

_____
_____
_____
_____
_____
_____
_____
_____
_____
_____
_____
_____
_____
_____
_____
_____
_____

Balance a checking account:

Another task that seems like a blast from the past. However, this is extremely important. Many people these days rely on the bank to keep an ongoing total of their money. Banks make mistakes and it's important to know how to keep track of your money. If you have outstanding checks that haven't been accounted for by your bank yet and you keep spending money that you thought was there, you can end up paying many fees.

Check books come with a register, as shown below. Some will fill it out as they spend money, while others will keep receipts and fill it out later. The latter leaves you with a higher chance of missing a receipt. Remember, this is your checking account and used for more than writing checks. Any ATM transaction, store purchase, or any other time you use your debit card should be recorded. Don't forget deposits, including when you get paid!

Fill the register line for each transaction completely, including the very right $, which is your ongoing money in your account. You will need to add and subtract as money comes in and goes out. The checkmark is if the bank cleared the check you wrote.

CHECK # OR CODE	DATE	TRANSACTION DESCRIPTION	PAYMENT AMOUNT	FEE	✓	DEPOSIT AMOUNT	$
			$			$	

LEARNING TO LIVE:

Life Skills for ALL Ages

Topic: Balance a checking account

Date Learned: _____

Date Reviewed: _____

Date Mastered: _____

What I learned:

_____
_____
_____
_____
_____
_____
_____
_____
_____
_____
_____
_____
_____
_____
_____
_____
_____
_____
_____

Credit Cards: *This is fictious. I'm not asking you to open a credit card.

Credit cards can come in handy, but they can also end you up in financial disaster. It's easy to say, "only spend what you currently have". However, sometimes that's not possible in emergency situations, i.e., if your car breaks down or your water heater breaks.

Credit card companies have some very tempting promotions, like you can get airline miles when you spend money on their card, or you can get gas discounts. Credit cards are helpful to build credit for when you need to buy a new vehicle or house so it is okay to use, but you must be careful.

It's on you to keep these in check. Always try to pay more than your minimum payment. It would be preferred if you made the full payment. When you pay a minimum, you are not knocking your payments down and only paying part of your monthly finance fees. These fees can really add up and you will never make headway on your money borrowed from the credit card, which in turn will leave you in constant debt.

If you find yourself in a situation where you cannot pay the card, call your credit card company and ask to have a break. They won't always help as this is their money they need back, but it's better than not paying at all. Any missed payments will result in hurting your credit score, which will be explained later in this chapter. It will also end up costing you even more money in the end.

For this exercise, pick two random credit cards and assume you have a balance of $500. All credit cards charge interest when there is a balance, and some will charge an annual fee. Check their benefits and interest rate (APR). As you compare these two cards, read the small print. Check all additional fees. What's your best option?

LEARNING TO LIVE:

Life Skills for ALL Ages

Topic: Credit Cards

Date Learned: _____

Date Reviewed: _____

Date Mastered: _____

What I learned:

_____
_____
_____
_____
_____
_____
_____
_____
_____
_____
_____
_____
_____
_____
_____
_____
_____

Loans:

Loans are similar to credit cards. The difference is a loan will be a chunk of money at once that is borrowed and you can't keep adding to it like you can a credit card. With a loan, you are borrowing a certain amount of money from a bank or institution and signing that you agree to pay it all back, usually by a certain date, while making monthly payments.

Popular loans are taken out for cars, houses, or education. You can also take out personal loans or the like. You would need to fill out an application and be approved. You may ask for a $25,000 loan but only approved for $20,000. The bank will approve or deny based on your credit score, to be explained in a later section. They will look at your history of borrowing money along with how much money you currently make. They want to make sure you will be able to pay their monthly payment without maxing you out. If your payment is too high, you won't be able to live either.

For this section's project, investigate a car loan and compare two different companies. Just like borrowing money for a credit card, check the interest rate difference. This may be more difficult as many rates will depend on your credit score. Read the fine print. There can be many hidden fees written into the small writing. Which one is better and why do you figure it's the better one to work with?

LEARNING TO LIVE:

Life Skills for ALL Ages

Topic: Loans

Date Learned: _____

Date Reviewed: _____

Date Mastered: _____

What I learned:

_____

_____

_____

_____

_____

_____

_____

_____

_____

_____

_____

_____

_____

_____

_____

_____

_____

_____

Paying Bills:

As an adult, or even an older teen, there will always be some sort of bill to pay and oftentimes many bills. Rent/mortgage, utilities, education, credit cards, loans, the list goes on and on. You will notice your bills aren't always due on the same date. Some may be on the 1st, others on the 15th, or some just randomly throughout the month. It is highly suggested to make yourself a bill pay spreadsheet to keep track of all bills coming out and when you must pay. Even if you set up electronic bill pay, you'll still need to plan for it to come out of your account.

In chapter two, a sample bill pay spreadsheet was given for your future living project. After all this time, that chapter is now becoming a reality. Make sure you budget your money appropriately. You do not want to pay all the bills in one cycle if you can avoid it, otherwise you may run out of money to feed yourself your put gas in your car to drive to work.

In this section, go back to chapter two and refresh work another bill pay checklist. Be sure at the end of each pay period, you are still positive in your money column.

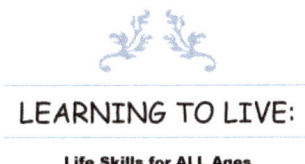

LEARNING TO LIVE:

Life Skills for ALL Ages

Topic: Paying Bills

Date Learned: _____

Date Reviewed: _____

Date Mastered: _____

What I learned:

_____
_____
_____
_____
_____
_____
_____
_____
_____
_____
_____
_____
_____
_____
_____
_____
_____

Late Fees:

It shouldn't be any surprise, but if you don't pay your bills on time, they will charge late fees. You may feel it's mean, but remember, these companies are counting on your money to pay their own bills as well. Late fees can be costly, and I know you would rather keep your money in your account rather than pay additional for it. If you continue to not pay there may be consequences i.e., turning off your electricity or water.

In this section look up two local utility companies. Check their late fees if the bill is not paid on time. Also, check their consequences if the bill is not paid in a timely manner. Again, like with all the companies you are doing business with, read the fine print.

LEARNING TO LIVE:

Life Skills for ALL Ages

Topic: Late Fees

Date Learned: _____

Date Reviewed: _____

Date Mastered: _____

What I learned:

_____
_____
_____
_____
_____
_____
_____
_____
_____
_____
_____
_____
_____
_____
_____
_____
_____

Credit Reports and Score:

A credit report will hold all personal information about you. It is a statement that shows your credit activity, current and historical credit situation, along with the status of your credit accounts. It will also have all the addresses you lived at, date of birth, social security number, phone numbers, liens, foreclosures, bankruptcies, etc. Companies you want to borrow money from will pull these reports before allowing you to be approved.

There are three major credit report agencies: Equifax, Experian, and TransUnion. Each of them holds their own reports and sometimes varies with your score.

A credit score can vary from 300-850. The higher the credit score, the higher the better. A higher score can give you more access to lower interest rates or higher borrowing amounts. It is important to know where you stand and can get your score pulled from a bank.

See below for credit score ratings.

- 720 or higher = excellent credit

- 690-719 = good credit

- 630-689 = fair credit

- 629 and lower = poor credit

*Creditors will set their own standards, but this is a general guideline.

LEARNING TO LIVE:

Life Skills for ALL Ages

Topic: Credit Reports and Score

Date Learned: _____

Date Reviewed: _____

Date Mastered: _____

What I learned:

_____
_____
_____
_____
_____
_____
_____
_____
_____
_____
_____
_____
_____
_____
_____
_____
_____
_____

Paying off debt:

It's very easy to get into a situation where you cannot pay for your needs during a certain month. Maybe an unexpected car repair bill came up, or you need groceries but changed jobs and have to wait for an additional two weeks until the next paycheck comes in, or maybe you were laid off from your job unexpectedly and live paycheck to paycheck. These are situations that commonly arise throughout the country. Having a credit card may look like the best option for that month or several months. While it's great to have in emergencies, still be careful using it or you could wind up in thousands of dollars in debt and try paying it off for years.

Calculate all your monthly bills. If you have more than one credit card, take a look at the interest rate. Try to talk to the creditors and consolidate those cards into one. This way if you have a $250 minimum payment to each card, you are paying $500 of mostly interest. If they are consolidated, your minimum payment may be $350 (since there's more debt on one card and none on the other). Still pay the $500 you normally would, but now $150 will go straight to the principal.

For this lesson, make a grid. If you have $15,000 in credit card debt at 30% interest rate monthly, how long will it take to pay off when paying $500 each month. It may seem like a very long time, but if you have a goal in mind, you can achieve a payoff. If you are only making minimum payments, your debt will sit there for decades.

LEARNING TO LIVE:

Life Skills for ALL Ages

Topic: Paying off Debt

Date Learned: _____

Date Reviewed: _____
Date Mastered: _____

What I learned:

_____
_____
_____
_____
_____
_____
_____
_____
_____
_____
_____
_____
_____
_____
_____
_____
_____

Taxes:

Taxes are a tough subject matter to discuss in just a page or two. You should always consult a tax professional for advice or questions, which I am not.

Taxes are due to the government on April 15th yearly. Employers are required to mail out your W2 no later than January 31st. This section will teach you how to read your W2. Please note, if you have worked at more than one company, you will receive one from each company.

a Employee's social security number		OMB No. 1545-0008	This information is being furnished to the Internal Revenue Service. If you are required to file a tax return, a negligence penalty or other sanction may be imposed on you if this income is taxable and you fail to report it.	
b Employer identification number (EIN)			1 Wages, tips, other compensation	2 Federal income tax withheld
c Employer's name, address, and ZIP code			3 Social security wages	4 Social security tax withheld
			5 Medicare wages and tips	6 Medicare tax withheld
			7 Social security tips	8 Allocated tips
d Control number			9	10 Dependent care benefits
e Employee's first name and initial Last name Suff.			11 Nonqualified plans	12a See instructions for box 12
			13 Statutory employee Retirement plan Third-party sick pay	12b
			14 Other	12c
				12d
f Employee's address and ZIP code				
15 State Employer's state ID number	16 State wages, tips, etc.	17 State income tax	18 Local wages, tips, etc.	19 Local income tax	20 Locality name

Form **W-2** Wage and Tax Statement   2021   Department of the Treasury—Internal Revenue Service

Copy C—For EMPLOYEE'S RECORDS   Safe, accurate, FAST! Use e~file

(See Notice to Employee on the back of Copy B.)

a Employee's social security number
This would be your own social security number that you provided back when you filled out your application for employment.

b Employer identification number (EIN)
The EIN that your company uses for you.

c Employer's name, address, and ZIP code

Your company's main office address information.

d Control number

Used by your company's payroll department. Some companies use this and some do not. If not, it will be left blank.

e Employee's first name and initial/Last name/Suff

This will be your information.

f Employee's address and zip

This will be your information.

1 Wages, tips, other compensation

This box will include all compensation you have received in the previous year from this company. Regular pay, overtime, tips, prizes that are taxable will be here. It will not include any deferrals to retirement plans or pretax benefits.

2 Federal income tax withheld

How much federal tax was withheld throughout the year. In some states, you elect this when you fill out your new hire paperwork.

3 Social security wages

Out of your entire wages, how much is subject to paying social security tax. The box may be higher or lower than box 1.

4 Social security tax withheld

The total you paid into social security tax for the year.

5 Medicare wages and tips

This number is likely higher than box 1. Medicare typically does not include any pretax deductions and will include most taxable benefits.

6 Medicare tax withheld

The amount of tax withheld for Medicare.

7 Social security tips

Tips that were reported by the employer.

8 Allocated tips

Tips your employer has attributed to you.

9 Verification Code

This code helps the IRS to verify if the W2 is authentic. This is a fairly new box on the W2, therefore, if it is not filled in, the IRS will still accept it.

10 Dependent Care Benefits

The total amount of benefits your employer paid under dependent care assistance.

11 Nonqualified plans

Any amount your employer paid you from a non-qualified compensation plan.

12 a-d

These are typically filled out if you are part of a 401(k) plan or employer paid health coverage. There are several different codes that can be used in these boxes.

13 Checkboxes

The employer will check mark the appropriate box for whichever type of employee you are.

14 Other

This box is to report anything that doesn't fit in any of the other boxes.

For this lesson, print out a blank 1040EZ form and fill it out completely. This is the easiest of tax forms. It's not to be used in a lot of situations, however, it's a great way to get the feel of what doing taxes are like.

LEARNING TO LIVE:

Life Skills for ALL Ages

Topic: Taxes

Date Learned: _____

Date Reviewed: _____

Date Mastered: _____

What I learned:

_____
_____
_____
_____
_____
_____
_____
_____
_____
_____
_____
_____
_____
_____
_____
_____
_____
_____
_____

Health is one of the most important topics. This chapter will discuss everything from the basics to keep yourself health to being your own advocate. While in school many moons ago, health class never taught me about insurance or being your own advocate and how important it is to fight for yourself if a doctor is not listening to your concerns. As an adult, most people are forced to figure it out on their own. This chapter will help ease you into the healthcare industry.

Personal Hygiene:

Each person's idea of what their personal hygiene is varies. However, here are some good tips that should be practiced on a daily basis.

Teeth: Brush twice a day (morning and night) for at least 2 minutes. It may seem like a long time, but set a timer and sing a song to yourself. Floss at least once daily, preferably at night, or use a waterpik to do the same job. Mouthwash at night is a great way to help prevent gum disease.

Hands: Wash your hands often in warm water with soap for at least 30 seconds. Always wash your hands after using the restroom, before and after handling food, after handling garbage, and after sneezing or blowing your nose. While hand sanitizers are good when in a bind; soap and water are always the best choice.

Bathing: Whether every day or every other day, it's important to keep yourself clean and smelling fresh. Always be sure to wash your hair, armpits, neck, stomach, knees, elbows, back, arms, and feet. Really every square inch of your body. When shampooing and conditioning your hair, it is extremely important to ensure everything gets rinsed out, otherwise once your hair dries, it will still look greasy.

Being clean will not only make you feel better about yourself, but it will also help prevent you from getting sick. By practicing good hygiene, your risk of getting lice, athlete's foot, and ringworm will be minimized.

In this lesson, go through the actions to show you know how to properly stay clean.

LEARNING TO LIVE:

Life Skills for ALL Ages

Topic: Personal Hygiene

Date Learned: _____

Date Reviewed: _____

Date Mastered: _____

What I learned:

_____

_____

_____

_____

_____

_____

_____

_____

_____

_____

_____

_____

_____

_____

_____

_____

_____

_____

Laundry:

Laundry is one of the most dreaded chores by many people. There are a few steps involved and it could take all day. The good thing is you have the opportunity to take several breaks in between. I highly recommend getting into a habit of doing the entire laundry in one day, otherwise it will be looming around you.

Separate: A great debate. Some people highly recommend separating lights from darks, and some just throw it all together. This is a personal choice, however, if you throw darks with lights, be careful of adding that new bright red shirt with the white underwear, or you will end up with pink underwear.

Wash: On your washer, select the correct settings, whether you have a small load or large. Do not overfill as it will not get your clothes as clean. Start your washer and add the detergent. I prefer adding detergent before clothes, so you don't end up with soap stains on your clothes. Yes, soap can stain. Close it up and let it do its job.

Dryer: Ensure the lint trap is empty and throw clothes from the washer to the dryer. Again, it will not dry all the way if you overload it. Throw in a dryer sheet and set the dryer.

Second batch: Most of the time, your laundry will be more than one load. Once you have the dryer going, your washer is now empty and ready for the next load to get started.

Folding: The dreaded folding and putting away of the laundry. My best suggestion is to make it a game. Fold as much as you can during a tv show and once it goes to commercial hurry up and put away. Repeat until all the laundry is done. I know, with all these streaming services now, there aren't many commercials. You can pause before the next show begins to put everything away.

Find out the best way to get yourself motivated to complete the laundry in one day. You will feel so much better if it doesn't sit in a laundry basket for a week. Please note: When doing laundry, you do not want to allow the washer to sit with wet clothes for too long. In time, the clothes will start to smell like mildew, and you will need to rewash everything again.

LEARNING TO LIVE:

Life Skills for ALL Ages

Topic: Laundry

Date Learned: _____

Date Reviewed: _____

Date Mastered: _____

What I learned:

_____

_____

_____

_____

_____

_____

_____

_____

_____

_____

_____

_____

_____

_____

_____

_____

_____

_____

_____

House cleaning:

House cleaning or another term you may hear often is chores. While sometimes dreaded, think of how much better you will feel in a clean house. Set yourself a schedule so it becomes a habit.

Sweeping/Mopping: Get a good broom and make sure you sweep under all furniture to get the dust and dirt out. Using a dustpan, sweep all debris into it and toss in the garbage. I personally always fight with the dustpan as it leaves streaks of dirt, no matter how many times I try. I prefer to use the vacuum hose to get all the little bits. After sweeping mop the same area. Make sure you don't leave any cleaner residue once done or your floors won't look clean.

Vacuuming: Vacuum all areas of carpet or rugs you may have. This includes on the stairs. Most vacuums come with an attachment specifically for stairs. Be careful while vacuuming the stairs as you don't want to fall.

Bathrooms: Follow the directions for the cleaners of your choice. Make sure to sweep, mop, clean the vanity, tub/shower, mirror, and most importantly the toilet.

Kitchen: Clean off all countertops and appliances. It's a good idea to get in the habit of cleaning these after you make a meal. This will prevent rodents and insects from coming in. Also wash and dry any dishes after eating.

Dusting: All surfaces, especially those that are wooden, need to be dusted. Make sure the cleaner you use is appropriate for the surface you are cleaning.

Spring cleaning: It doesn't really have to be in spring, but many people find the change in weather a motivator to get the house deep cleaned. This is that perfect opportunity to clean surfaces that don't typically get touched. Possibly behind the appliances, on top shelves that get ignored, or even cleaning out the closets or organizing the garage.

In this lesson, pinpoint all areas of the home that need to be cleaned often, whether weekly or biweekly. Make a schedule and decide what days you prefer to do which chores. Once you do the above chores have a parent look at your work. Take their feedback on anything you may have missed. It's the perfect opportunity to get better. Living in a clean environment will not only help you feel better but can also help prevent you from getting sick.

LEARNING TO LIVE:

Life Skills for ALL Ages

Topic: House cleaning

Date Learned: _____

Date Reviewed: _____

Date Mastered: _____

What I learned:

_____

_____

_____

_____

_____

_____

_____

_____

_____

_____

_____

_____

_____

_____

_____

_____

Sexual Education:

This book will often be used with a parent and their child. Everyone has different views on this subject, and I will not give my views on it. However, I have included this topic in the book, because of its great importance.

In this section, I would like for the parent to personally go over this subject matter with their child. In the learned/reviewed/mastered section ask the child what was discussed and make sure they are understanding.

LEARNING TO LIVE:

Life Skills for ALL Ages

Topic: Sexual Education

Date Learned: _____

Date Reviewed: _____

Date Mastered: _____

What I learned:

_____

_____

_____

_____

_____

_____

_____

_____

_____

_____

_____

_____

_____

_____

_____

Health Insurance:

Your employer may offer health insurance where they pay a portion of the cost, and you pay the rest in your paycheck. You may be getting your insurance on your own without an employer. Either way, health insurance is highly suggested to have. You never know when you may get sick or injured, plus having health insurance can also help keep you healthy by having your annual checkups. The amount you pay for insurance is just that. It's for the insurance itself and will help with the doctors' bills.

Copay: A copay is a fixed amount you pay at the time of service. Oftentimes, the copay amount is listed on your insurance card. A copayment is often a different amount for an office visit versus an emergency visit. Depending on your insurance, it may or may not be counted towards your deductible.

Coinsurance: This will be a percentage of how much you will owe the provider. For example, if you have an 80/20 plan. That means insurance will pay 80% of your visit and you will be responsible for the remaining 20%. This will be billed at a later date after the insurance has been billed. The catch is, this does not go into effect until the deductible is met.

Deductible: This is the amount you pay before insurance will start paying. For example, if your deductible is $1,000, you will pay all bills fully. Once you have hit $1,000 during the insurance term (typically January 1-December 31), then you will pay 20% of all remaining bills.

Out of Pocket: Using the examples above, if your out-of-pocket maximum is $5000, this is the most you will pay for the year. Insurance will then pay anything above that.

Full example: Sally went to the doctor and paid a $25 copay which does not count towards her deductible. She later receives a bill for $500 for services that were rendered at that appointment. She is responsible to pay that bill in full. She then had a surgery which cost $10,000. She will pay her remaining $500 in full to make it to her $1,000 deductible. From $1,000 to $5,000 she will pay 20% of the cost. The remaining $5,000 the insurance will pay in full along with any other doctor appointments she may have for the year.

It can get confusing, but you are always able to call your insurance company to make sure you understand your insurance completely. You may also reach out to your Human Resources department if you have your insurance through your employer.

In Network/Out of Network: To add another layer on top, providers have agreements with insurance companies, and they may or may not accept your insurance. If the provider accepts your insurance, that would be "In Network". If the provider has not negotiated a rate with your insurance company, it would be considered "Out of Network". If you are seen by an "Out of Network" provider, your insurance may not cover any of your visit. Always check with your insurance that your provider is covered.

In this section, look at health insurance cards from family and friends. See if you can read if there is a copay or what their deductible may be. Explain what each definition is and see what examples you can come up with.

LEARNING TO LIVE:

Life Skills for ALL Ages

Topic: Health Insurance

Date Learned: _____

Date Reviewed: _____

Date Mastered: _____

What I learned:

_____
_____
_____
_____
_____
_____
_____
_____
_____
_____
_____
_____
_____
_____
_____
_____

Your own advocate:

Being an advocate for yourself in healthcare means you raise awareness to your provider regarding any issues you may be having. You are the only one that truly knows what pain or symptoms you are experiencing, make sure it is known. There is nothing to be embarrassed about, this is the only way the provider can address your concerns. Remember if your provider does not believe you or writes off what you are saying, you have the right to a second opinion. Make an appointment with another doctor's office. Sometimes it takes a couple of tries to find someone who is also in your corner. Doctors don't know everything, and some will have experience with your symptoms that others may not. The biggest take away is to not be timid and speak up.

In this section, practice with a parent or peer. It is important to use describing words for what your symptoms are. With this practice, it will help for when you truly need to advocate for yourself.

LEARNING TO LIVE:

Life Skills for ALL Ages

Topic: Your own advocate

Date Learned: _____

Date Reviewed: _____

Date Mastered: _____

What I learned:

_____
_____
_____
_____
_____
_____
_____
_____
_____
_____
_____
_____
_____
_____
_____
_____
_____
_____

Medical Background:

Knowledge of your medical background and family history is so important if you are able to obtain it. Typically, knowing both parents, siblings, and grandparents history is what doctors need to be aware of. Many illnesses are genetic meaning they are passed down throughout family members. My daughter is adopted and not knowing her family medical history is sometimes a challenge.

For this section, make a spreadsheet and document any illnesses or diseases you have been diagnosed with along with your closest family members. Keep this in a place you can refer to any time you are ready to head to a doctor's office. Every year make sure to go back and update this document as things may have changed. Keeping this document will help doctors for any issues you may be sharing with them.

LEARNING TO LIVE:

Life Skills for ALL Ages

Topic: Medical Background

Date Learned: _____

Date Reviewed: _____

Date Mastered: _____

What I learned:

_____
_____
_____
_____
_____
_____
_____
_____
_____
_____
_____
_____
_____
_____
_____
_____
_____
_____

Making Doctors' Appointments:

Sometimes it can be intimidating to make a doctor's appointment as the receptionist or appointment setter may ask several questions. Be prepared with your personal calendar handy. Specialists tend to schedule further out and could be months before you're able to be seen. Having your calendar handy will allow you to see if you already have an engagement on that date. You don't want to wait several months to be seen, only to realize later that it will need to be rescheduled because you already had an event happening at that same time. General practitioners typically can get you in sooner within days.

If you do have to reschedule a doctor's appointment, be sure to give them as much notice as possible. Some offices will charge you for a full visit if you cancel less than 24 hours out.

Have your insurance card with you while on the phone. Typically, when making an appointment you will be asked for your insurance policy number, group number if applicable, and on the back of the card the PO Box claims need to be sent to. They will also ask why you are needing to be seen. Again, if it's a sensitive issue, don't be embarrassed. You are speaking with professionals.

In this lesson, set up a personal calendar and enter all appointments or obligations. With everything on your calendar, you will be able to prevent overbooking yourself.

LEARNING TO LIVE:

Life Skills for ALL Ages

Topic: Making Doctors' Appointments

Date Learned: _____

Date Reviewed: _____

Date Mastered: _____

What I learned:

_____

_____

_____

_____

_____

_____

_____

_____

_____

_____

_____

_____

_____

_____

_____

_____

CPR:

It is highly recommended to take a class on CPR and first aid that will certify you at the end. CPR (Cardiopulmonary Resuscitation) is an emergency lifesaving procedure performed if the victim's heart stops pumping. CPR is a critical step in keeping the blow flow going to the heart before first responders arrive.

CPR is made up of chest compressions and mouth to mouth resuscitation (breathing). While getting ready to perform CPR, make sure someone is calling 9-1-1.

1. Lay the victim on their back with their head slightly tipped back to open their airway.
2. Check to see if they are breathing by putting your ear towards their mouth. If not, begin CPR.
3. Perform 30 chest compressions with your hands together and below their rib cage.
4. Give 2 rescue breaths into the victim's mouth.
5. Repeat until first responders arrive or the victim starts breathing on their own.

Often times, an AED (automated external defibrillator) is available in public locations. Have someone bring that to you. Once it is turned on, it will walk you through how to use it.

For this lesson, register and attend a CPR and first aid class. These classes are a few hours long and will teach you how to properly use CPR. CPR certification is usually good for about 2 years before it needs to be renewed.

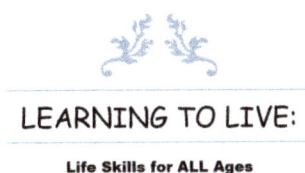

LEARNING TO LIVE:

Life Skills for ALL Ages

Topic: CPR

Date Learned: _____

Date Reviewed: _____

Date Mastered: _____

What I learned:

_____
_____
_____
_____
_____
_____
_____
_____
_____
_____
_____
_____
_____
_____
_____
_____
_____
_____

Basic First Aid:

While in the CPR class, most companies off a first aid class at the same time. First aid can include cleaning minor cuts and scrapes, treating minor burns, blisters, and applying bandages and so much more.

Applying bandages for a cut: Always clean the wound with warm water and antibacterial soap. Place the cloth part of the bandage over the wound and gently, not tightly, attach the sticky sides to the skin.

Applying bandages for sprains: Wrap the bandage firmly, not tightly, around the affected area. Attach with a safety pin or bandage clip. Ask the patient if the bandage is too tight, if it is, they will begin to lose circulation in the affected area and will need to redo the bandage. You can check the circulation by pressing a fingernail into the skin until the skin goes pale. If the color does not return right away, it may be too tight. Check the circulation often as when the limb swells, it could end up losing circulation later on.

Treating a minor burn: The most important thing to start is to cool the burn. Use either running water or a compress. Make sure it is cool, but not cold. Do not use ice as this will cause more damage. If a blister occurs, do not break it. Apply aloe vera or a moisturizer. Bandage the burn with sterile gauze. If necessary, over the counter pain medication can be taken orally.

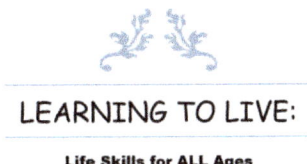

LEARNING TO LIVE:

Life Skills for ALL Ages

Topic: Basic First Aid

Date Learned: _____

Date Reviewed: _____

Date Mastered: _____

What I learned:

_____
_____
_____
_____
_____
_____
_____
_____
_____
_____
_____
_____
_____
_____
_____
_____
_____
_____

Chapter Nine:
Other Hot Topics

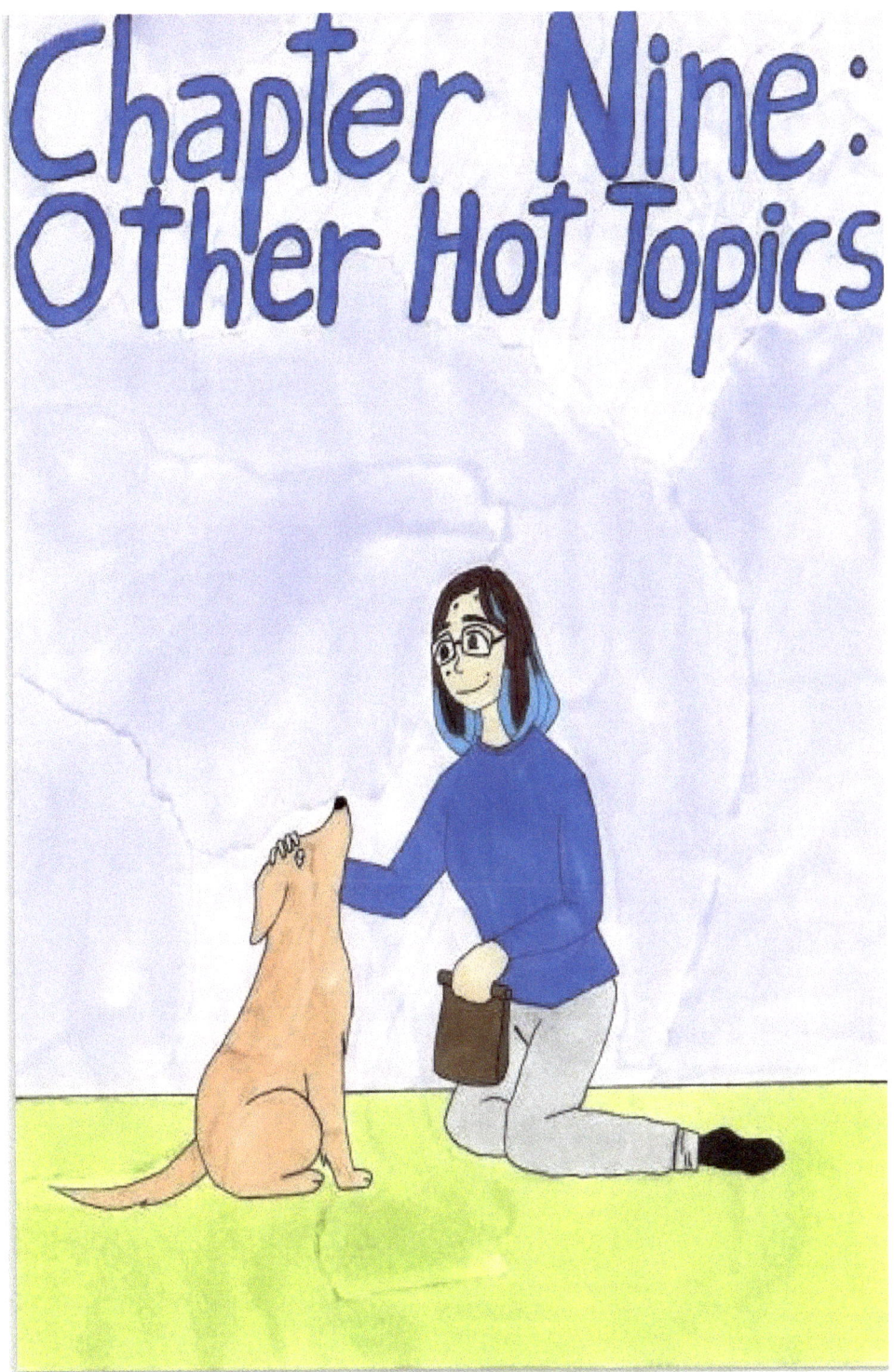

There are so many topics that can be covered on things that should be known, but it would be impossible to cover them all. In this chapter I am covering some topics that don't quite fit into the other chapters. Again, in the next chapter there are extra pages to be filled out for anything that is important in your family that wasn't covered here.

Using a Public Restroom:

Once children come to a certain age, parents may feel it is time to allow the child to go into the restroom by themselves. This is more so for fathers/daughters or mothers/sons as they may have to go to the restrooms separately.

1. Wait in line if there is one. No one wants to be cut in front of when waiting to use the restroom.
2. Do not talk to strangers. Be aware of your surroundings.
3. Boys have a choice of a urinal or a stall while girls will have just the stall. Once entering, make sure to lock the door behind you.
4. Treat the restroom better than your own. Do not leave toilet paper on the floor or seat. If using a seat protector, be sure to throw it away. Girls of age need to dispose of their feminine products in the waste receptacle.
5. Once done with business, wash hands with warm water and soap. Be sure to dry.
6. When leaving the restroom, meet your parent in the exact place they advised.

For this lesson, do some practice runs at home and then go into public. Start with a less busy public restroom before going to one at an event or similar.

LEARNING TO LIVE:

Life Skills for ALL Ages

Topic: Using a public restroom

Date Learned: _____

Date Reviewed: _____

Date Mastered: _____

What I learned:

_____
_____
_____
_____
_____
_____
_____
_____
_____
_____
_____
_____
_____
_____
_____
_____
_____
_____

Dating Etiquette:

Keeping yourself safe while dating is essential. I cannot tell you the appropriate age for dating as this is a family decision. It is encouraged to meet in a public location, maybe a mall, or maybe a restaurant, or maybe even go on a double date with friends. It would be preferred that the parents meet the other and always know where the date will be held at. Both parties of the date should remain respectful. Treat others as you like to be treated, don't talk down to them and never touch in a mean way. Enjoy each other's company. Discuss with each other who will pay. Will one pay for dinner and the other pay for the activity. Will your own way the whole time.

No means no. If there is something that you do not want to do, the other party needs to understand and respect your decision. For example, if they ask to kiss you and you say no, you shouldn't have to explain yourself or be pressured into it. Be respectful of yourself and allow your limits to be heard.

For this lesson, come up with your own dating rules. Decide what you would be comfortable with and what is going to far. Have a discussion with your parents regarding this and make sure you are both on the same wavelength.

LEARNING TO LIVE:

Life Skills for ALL Ages

Topic: Dating Etiquette

Date Learned: _____

Date Reviewed: _____

Date Mastered: _____

What I learned:

_____

_____

_____

_____

_____

_____

_____

_____

_____

_____

_____

_____

_____

_____

_____

_____

_____

_____

Bullying:

Bullying is a serious topic with most school's having a zero tolerance policy. If you are bullied, say something. If you witness bullying, say something. Bullying is when one person or a group of people are seeking harm or intimidating someone else. It can be name calling or hitting or anything in between and is typically thrown at someone they see as vulnerable. Bullies tend to have low self-esteem and feel they need to dominate and cause others to have low self-esteem as well.

If you witness a bully or become a victim of a bully, you should:

1. Look at that person and calmly ask them to stop.
2. Walk away.
3. Tell an adult immediately.
4. Don't allow hurtful words to bring you down.
5. Learn self defense (see later in the book).
6. Be kind to the person that is the victim of the bully. Knowing they have a friend in you will help.

In this lesson, practice what you would do. It's not always easy to stand up to a bully and there may be a fear that you will become the next one bullied. If no one stops the bully, he/she will begin to think it's okay and will continue to do so. Help spread kindness and be the change.

LEARNING TO LIVE:

Life Skills for ALL Ages

Topic: Bullying

Date Learned: _____

Date Reviewed: _____

Date Mastered: _____

What I learned:

_____

_____

_____

_____

_____

_____

_____

_____

_____

_____

_____

_____

_____

_____

_____

_____

Social Media:

Social Media can be viewed as a great resource for connecting family and friends or expressing yourself, however it can also be viewed in a negative light for cyber bullying and more. It is very important to take great care when using social media platforms.

1. Treat others as you would like to be treated. Always be nice and avoid cyber bullying.
2. Think about what you post before you post it. Reread what you are sending and think about how others may view it.
3. Be true to you. Always be your own person. You don't have to pretend to be anything you are not just to fit in.
4. Do not accept friend requests from people you do not know.
5. Never send inappropriate pictures or engage in appropriate conversations.

Always keep yourself safe on the internet and parents should always keep a watchful eye on what is being posted, conversations that are being had, and how social media is affecting the child. Taking a social media break every once in a while is a great idea as well. Social media has become a hard habit to break, and occasional breaks are needed.

For this lesson, have a parent read off some social media posts. Decide if it is appropriate or inappropriate. What makes it appropriate or inappropriate? How would you feel if you saw a post like this? How might you reply to a post like this?

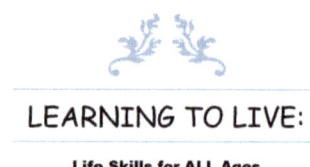

LEARNING TO LIVE:

Life Skills for ALL Ages

Topic: Social Media

Date Learned: _____

Date Reviewed: _____

Date Mastered: _____

What I learned:

_____

_____

_____

_____

_____

_____

_____

_____

_____

_____

_____

_____

_____

_____

_____

_____

_____

World Wide Web:

The internet, just like social media, can be a great source of helpful information and a wide variety of knowledge. Again, it can also be a terrible place to go down the rabbit hole of negativity. It is important to teach how to look up information and what links to click on and what to avoid.

1. Always make sure your internet connection is secure with a strong password that only the household knows.
2. Parents should often check user history to verify the websites that have been visited.
3. Review your privacy settings so hackers cannot break in.
4. Use a good anti-virus software.
5. Practice safe browsing.
6. Do not click on pop up ads or web search ads.
7. Do not give your personal information unless you are positive it is a true website and not a scam.

For this lesson, with a parent, use a search engine and look up some topics you would like to know more information about. What links would you click on a why? Do they appear safe? Are they truly safe?

LEARNING TO LIVE:

Life Skills for ALL Ages

Topic: World Wide Web

Date Learned: _____

Date Reviewed: _____

Date Mastered: _____

What I learned:

_____
_____
_____
_____
_____
_____
_____
_____
_____
_____
_____
_____
_____
_____
_____
_____
_____

Self-Defense:

Why is learning self-defense so important? Just like you are now your own advocate; you want to protect your body as well. If someone is trying to grab a hold of you without your permission or if someone is trying to snag your wallet. Hopefully you will never have to use it, but it's something that you should know. Self-defense isn't just learning how to kick and scream, it's also in the power of the mind.

1. **Trust your instincts.** If something doesn't feel right, it probably isn't. Move towards an area with more people nearby.
2. **Do not make yourself a target.** Be aware of your surroundings. Do not stare at your phone as you walk and lose sense of what is around you.
3. **Show confidence.** Predators will be less likely to approach you if you're showing signs of confidence. If you look confused, distracted, or scared, they are more likely to target you.
4. **Keep it simple.** No matter what techniques you decide to use in martial arts, keep it simple, to the point and don't panic.

For this lesson, look up some simple techniques to learn that would be suitable for you. Practice, not on a person, but on a stuffed animal or similar. Stay safe out there.

LEARNING TO LIVE:

Life Skills for ALL Ages

Topic: Self-Defense

Date Learned: _____

Date Reviewed: _____

Date Mastered: _____

What I learned:

_____

_____

_____

_____

_____

_____

_____

_____

_____

_____

_____

_____

_____

_____

_____

_____

_____

Pumping Gas:

There are still a few states that have laws which you are not allowed to pump your own gas, so we'll assume you're not from those states. It is recommended and sometimes law, depending on your state, for no one to pump gas until they are a licensed driver, or age 16. I didn't realize that until I was reading it on a pump one day. Reason being is fumes are unsafe for younger children and burns can happen easily. Even if you are currently under that age, gas safety is still an important skill.

1. Turn off vehicle prior to pumping gas.
2. Do not reenter the car while fueling. There is a greater issue for static to cause a fire if you reenter. If you must go back into the vehicle, discharge any possible static by touching the outside of the vehicle.
3. You will need to pay inside with cash or at the pump with a credit or debit card.
4. Know what side your tank is on. When looking at the gas gauge on the dashboard, next the "E" will have an arrow. This arrow points to the side the tank is.
5. Verify what octane gas works best with the car. If you are unsure, check the car's user manual.
6. Lock all doors when you exit your vehicle to ensure no one can steal from inside the car.
7. Do not "top off" the tank. Once the pump stops fueling, shake off the excess drops into the tank and put the pump back.
8. Ensure the gas cap is fully secured.
9. Do not smoke or have fire near the gas pumps.
10. If a fire occurs, leave the pump nozzle inside and immediately notify a gas attendant. They will be able to turn off the gas.

For this lesson, ensure you remember the above.

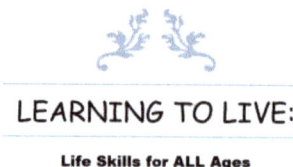

LEARNING TO LIVE:

Life Skills for ALL Ages

Topic: Pumping Gas

Date Learned: _____

Date Reviewed: _____

Date Mastered: _____

What I learned:

_____
_____
_____
_____
_____
_____
_____
_____
_____
_____
_____
_____
_____
_____
_____
_____
_____

Maintaining a car:

With owning a car comes maintaining the car. Find a good mechanic or learn to work on cars so if something goes wrong it can be fixed. However, for basic maintenance there are some things you'll need to know.

1. Inspect and maintain tires. Make sure there are no nails, and the tires are filled to the proper weight.
2. Get an oil change every 3,000 miles or so to keep it running its best life.
3. Change your engine air filter.
4. Check all fluids: brake, oil, power steering, and transmission.
5. Test your headlights and brake lights. Having lights out is not only illegal, but it can also hinder seeing while driving.
6. Replace your windshield wipers when they no longer work as well as they once did. You do not want to be stuck in a storm and unable to see because of bad wipers.
7. Check your brakes. Take your vehicle in and have them test your brakes. If the brakes go out, it will be a very scary situation.
8. Wash your car. It can maintain the paint job and undercarriage to get all road materials and debris away.
9. Check belts and hoses.

For this section, learn this list as a minimum. It's a great start to properly maintaining your vehicle and running smoothly so you avoid getting stuck on the road.

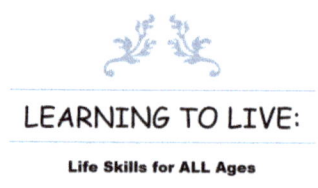

LEARNING TO LIVE:

Life Skills for ALL Ages

Topic: Maintaining a car

Date Learned: _____

Date Reviewed: _____

Date Mastered: _____

What I learned:

_____
_____
_____
_____
_____
_____
_____
_____
_____
_____
_____
_____
_____
_____
_____
_____
_____
_____

Pulled over by police:

It can be a scary thing if you are pulled over by a police officer. You should be prepared if this happens to you. Parents, please have a conversation with your child about this topic as well.

1. Carefully choose where to stop. Safety first, you want to pull all the way to the right off the road. If there is not a place to stop, then look for a gas station or neighborhood you can pull into.
2. Remain calm. Take a deep breath and listen to what the officer is asking. Typically, they will ask for a driver's license, proof of insurance, and registration.
3. Don't reach for anything without advising the officer. Keep in mind sudden movements may make the officer think you are reaching for a weapon.
4. Do not give excuses. The last thing officers want to hear is a bunch of excuses.
5. Watch your voice. Do not raise your voice to the officer as it can come off as combative.

For this lesson, role play with a parent for different instances. If you were pulled over in a vehicle for speeding, because you match the description of someone they are looking for, and because you are out past curfew.

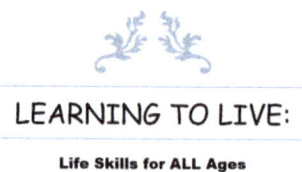

LEARNING TO LIVE:

Life Skills for ALL Ages

Topic: Being pulled over by police

Date Learned: _____

Date Reviewed: _____

Date Mastered: _____

What I learned:

_____
_____
_____
_____
_____
_____
_____
_____
_____
_____
_____
_____
_____
_____
_____
_____
_____
_____

Keeping a pet:

What type of pet are you interested in? A pet mouse, hamster, fish, dog, cat, and the list goes on. What makes you excited thinking about owning a pet? The first step is to research the pet you are interested in. Find out what habitat (or cage) they may need, what food they need, and what is needed to keep them healthy, for example, taking your animal to the vet.

Owning a pet is a family decision. There needs to be a person dedicated to feeding, taking them outside or cleaning up after them, play with the animal and all other needs that come with it.

For this lesson, choose an animal of your choice and create an argument for why that pet is important to join the household. Present this argument to your whole family. Again, this is just the assignment, and no one is telling you to get a pet. This is strictly for learning.

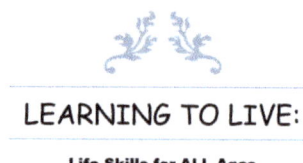

LEARNING TO LIVE:

Life Skills for ALL Ages

Topic: Keeping a pet

Date Learned: _____

Date Reviewed: _____

Date Mastered: _____

What I learned:

_____
_____
_____
_____
_____
_____
_____
_____
_____
_____
_____
_____
_____
_____
_____
_____
_____

165

Staying organized:

Why is it important to become and stay organized? It can benefit you living a happy and healthy life. It can also make you feel more less stressed, relaxed and calm.

1. **Set goals.** I prefer using a checklist and cross out as you complete tasks. Use a notebook to keep your checklists in so you don't have paper everywhere. To keep the checklist extra clean, once many items become crossed off, rewrite the whole list of everything you have left. On this checklist, write down what needs to be done. Use separate checklists for home and work.

2. **Use an agenda.** Agendas or even online calendars can help you keep track of activities and important to do's.

3. **Make a space for everything.** Whether it's hanging all shirts or having a spot for important papers. Everything should have their own home. When something is out of its home, that's when mess can start to accumulate. The use of labels on boxes for smaller items can help you remember what is in there.

4. **Keep a clean environment.** Whether it's your workstation or your bedroom, if it gets messy, your stress level will go up. It only takes a few minutes to put everything in its place but could take hours if you allow it to get messy.

5. **Take breaks.** When cleaning or going through a whole reorganization, it is important to take breaks throughout. This will help you reduce your burnout. However, if you're trying to get something finished before bedtime, make sure to limit how long each break is. You don't want a five-minute break to turn into an hour, and then lose all motivation to get back to it.

6. **Declutter.** One of the many reasons your organized life can become unorganized is because there's so much stuff. Declutter and donate or throw away anything you don't use. If you haven't used it in a year, chances are you never will.

For this lesson, pick an area of your life you feel needs to have more organization. Think of ways you can become and keep it organized. Now put it into action.

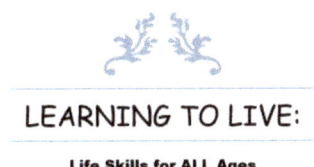

LEARNING TO LIVE:

Life Skills for ALL Ages

Topic: Staying organized:

Date Learned: _____

Date Reviewed: _____

Date Mastered: _____

What I learned:

_____
_____
_____
_____
_____
_____
_____
_____
_____
_____
_____
_____
_____
_____
_____
_____
_____
_____

Importance of Individuality:

Be who you are meant to be. It is okay to be different. What is normal anyways? No two people are the same, no one is "normal". Do not pretend to be someone you are not when you are around friends or family. In order to live your happiest life, you need to be true to yourself. People will accept you for who you are and if they don't, then maybe it is them with the problem and not yourself.

With this lesson, there is not a mastery sheet. Instead, just an area for you to write what you have learned about yourself. Go to a room where you can be alone with your thoughts. Think of who you are, why you love who you are, and what makes you so unique. Anytime you are feeling self-doubt, find that quiet space or somewhere you would consider your happy place and reflect. You are special, you are unique, you are your best self when you accept yourself.

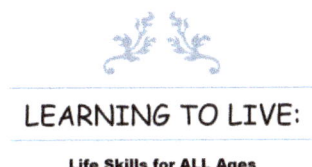

LEARNING TO LIVE:

Life Skills for ALL Ages

Topic: Importance of Individuality

What I learned:

_____

_____

_____

_____

_____

_____

_____

_____

_____

_____

_____

_____

_____

_____

_____

_____

_____

THE END!!!

You have made it to the end of the book! What an accomplishment! I hope you have enjoyed your time with each of these lessons. Keep this book for future reference as it will come in handy during your journey of life.

All items in this book are for fictional use. For additional learning to live mastery sheets, please see Chapter Ten. These sheets are great for anything that is important to your family that may not have been covered in the book.

LEARNING TO LIVE:

Life Skills for ALL Ages

Topic:

Date Learned: _____

Date Reviewed: _____

Date Mastered: _____

What I learned:

_____
_____
_____
_____
_____
_____
_____
_____
_____
_____
_____
_____
_____
_____
_____
_____
_____
_____
_____

LEARNING TO LIVE:

Life Skills for ALL Ages

Topic:

Date Learned: _____

Date Reviewed: _____

Date Mastered: _____

What I learned:

_____
_____
_____
_____
_____
_____
_____
_____
_____
_____
_____
_____
_____
_____
_____
_____
_____
_____
_____

LEARNING TO LIVE:

Life Skills for ALL Ages

Topic:

Date Learned: _____

Date Reviewed: _____

Date Mastered: _____

What I learned:

_____
_____
_____
_____
_____
_____
_____
_____
_____
_____
_____
_____
_____
_____
_____
_____
_____
_____

LEARNING TO LIVE:

Life Skills for ALL Ages

Topic:

Date Learned: _____

Date Reviewed: _____

Date Mastered: _____

What I learned:

_____
_____
_____
_____
_____
_____
_____
_____
_____
_____
_____
_____
_____
_____
_____
_____
_____
_____

LEARNING TO LIVE:

Life Skills for ALL Ages

Topic:

Date Learned: _____

Date Reviewed: _____

Date Mastered: _____

What I learned:

_____

_____

_____

_____

_____

_____

_____

_____

_____

_____

_____

_____

_____

_____

_____

_____

_____

LEARNING TO LIVE:

Life Skills for ALL Ages

Topic:

Date Learned: _____

Date Reviewed: _____

Date Mastered: _____

What I learned:

_____

_____

_____

_____

_____

_____

_____

_____

_____

_____

_____

_____

_____

_____

_____

_____

_____

_____

LEARNING TO LIVE:

Life Skills for ALL Ages

Topic:

Date Learned: _____

Date Reviewed: _____

Date Mastered: _____

What I learned:

_____
_____
_____
_____
_____
_____
_____
_____
_____
_____
_____
_____
_____
_____
_____
_____
_____
_____

LEARNING TO LIVE:

Life Skills for ALL Ages

Topic:

Date Learned: _____

Date Reviewed: _____

Date Mastered: _____

What I learned:

_____
_____
_____
_____
_____
_____
_____
_____
_____
_____
_____
_____
_____
_____
_____
_____

LEARNING TO LIVE:

Life Skills for ALL Ages

Topic:

Date Learned: _____

Date Reviewed: _____

Date Mastered: _____

What I learned:

_____
_____
_____
_____
_____
_____
_____
_____
_____
_____
_____
_____
_____
_____
_____
_____
_____

LEARNING TO LIVE:

Life Skills for ALL Ages

Topic:

Date Learned: _____

Date Reviewed: _____

Date Mastered: _____

What I learned:

_____
_____
_____
_____
_____
_____
_____
_____
_____
_____
_____
_____
_____
_____
_____
_____
_____
_____

LEARNING TO LIVE:

Life Skills for ALL Ages

Topic:

Date Learned: _____

Date Reviewed: _____

Date Mastered: _____

What I learned:

_____
_____
_____
_____
_____
_____
_____
_____
_____
_____
_____
_____
_____
_____
_____
_____
_____
_____

LEARNING TO LIVE:

Life Skills for ALL Ages

Topic:

Date Learned: _____

Date Reviewed: _____

Date Mastered: _____

What I learned:

_____
_____
_____
_____
_____
_____
_____
_____
_____
_____
_____
_____
_____
_____
_____
_____
_____
_____

LEARNING TO LIVE:

Life Skills for ALL Ages

Topic:

Date Learned: _____

Date Reviewed: _____

Date Mastered: _____

What I learned:

_____

_____

_____

_____

_____

_____

_____

_____

_____

_____

_____

_____

_____

_____

_____

_____

LEARNING TO LIVE:

Life Skills for ALL Ages

Topic:

Date Learned: _____

Date Reviewed: _____

Date Mastered: _____

What I learned:

_____
_____
_____
_____
_____
_____
_____
_____
_____
_____
_____
_____
_____
_____
_____
_____
_____

LEARNING TO LIVE:

Life Skills for ALL Ages

Topic:

Date Learned: _____

Date Reviewed: _____

Date Mastered: _____

What I learned:

_____
_____
_____
_____
_____
_____
_____
_____
_____
_____
_____
_____
_____
_____
_____
_____
_____
_____

LEARNING TO LIVE:

Life Skills for ALL Ages

Topic:

Date Learned: _____

Date Reviewed: _____

Date Mastered: _____

What I learned:

_____
_____
_____
_____
_____
_____
_____
_____
_____
_____
_____
_____
_____
_____
_____
_____
_____
_____

www.ingramcontent.com/pod-product-compliance
Lightning Source LLC
Chambersburg PA
CBHW051621120626
46551CB00014B/1897